World of Wonder
LIVING WORLD

SALARIYA

Published in Great Britain in 2008
by Book House, an imprint of
The Salariya Book Company Ltd
25 Marlborough Place,
Brighton BN1 1UB

Author: Gerard Cheshire has written
many books on natural history, and over
the past twelve years has cultivated an
excellent reputation as an author and
editor. He now lives in Bath, England,
with his wife and three sons.

Artists: Janet Baker (JB Illustrations),
Mark Bergin, John Francis,
Nick Hewetson, Pam Hewetson,
Li Sidong, Emily Mayer, Terry Riley,
Carolyn Scrace

Editor: Stephen Haynes

HB ISBN: 978-1-906370-46-6
PB ISBN: 978-1-906370-47-3

A CIP catalogue record for this book
is available from the British Library.

Printed and bound in China.

PAPER FROM
SUSTAINABLE
FORESTS

Visit our website at **www.salariya.com**
for **free** electronic versions of:

You Wouldn't Want to be an Egyptian Mummy!
You Wouldn't Want to be a Roman Gladiator!
Avoid Joining Shackleton's Polar Expedition!
Avoid Sailing on a 19th-Century Whaling Ship!

Sperm whale

World of Wonder
Living World

by

Gerard Cheshire

Spur-winged goose

Ostrich

BOOK HOUSE

Contents

Why is the living world special?

Tropical rainforest

The world around us is filled with living things. So far there are 1.7 million **species** known to science, and they come in all shapes and sizes, colours and patterns. Without the different animals and plants that make up the living world, we humans could not survive.

Rainforests have more species than any other kind of **habitat**. In fact, new species are being discovered every year.

What's the biggest creature on Earth?

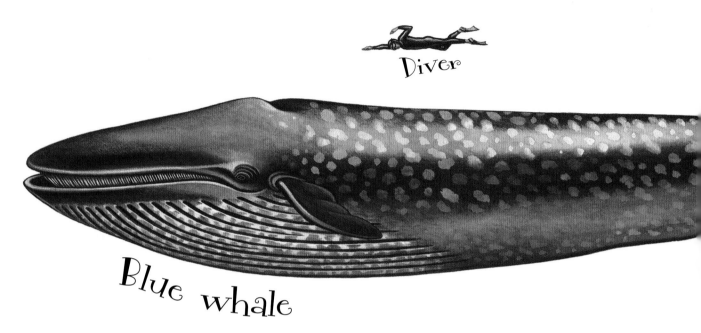

Diver

Blue whale

The blue whale is the biggest animal on earth. Even the giant dinosaurs didn't grow as large as the blue whale. The blue whale lives in the ocean, and the water helps to carry its huge weight. The blue whale can grow up to 33 metres long and weigh 180 tonnes.

Reticulated python

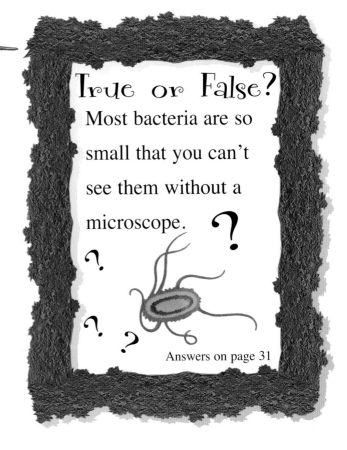

The reticulated python is one of the world's longest snakes, and can grow up to 7 metres long.

True or False?

Most bacteria are so small that you can't see them without a microscope.

Answers on page 31

African elephant

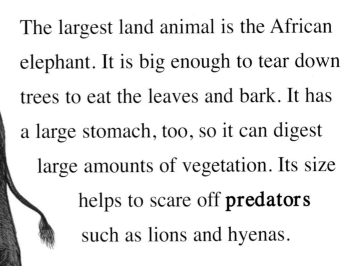

The largest land animal is the African elephant. It is big enough to tear down trees to eat the leaves and bark. It has a large stomach, too, so it can digest large amounts of vegetation. Its size helps to scare off **predators** such as lions and hyenas.

What are the fastest animals on Earth?

The fastest land animal is the cheetah. This big cat hunts fast-moving animals like antelope. A cheetah's top speed is about 130 km (80 miles) per hour, but it can run quickly only for a minute or so. After that, it has to slow down and rest.

Sailfish

What's the fastest fish?

The sailfish is the world's fastest fish. It can swim up to 105 km (65 miles) per hour when hunting. When a sailfish swims very fast, it folds down the sail-like fin on its back so that it can slip through the water more easily.

Cheetah

A need for speed!

Predators are animals that eat other animals.
Some predators use their great speed to chase
their **prey**. Other predators ambush their prey –
they creep up on them and strike by surprise.

Killer whale

The killer whale, or orca, is one of the fastest animals
in the ocean. It can swim at about 65 km (40 miles)
per hour. Killer whales swim thousands of kilometres
looking for food such as seals and fish. They can be
found in all of the world's oceans.

What's the tallest creature ever?

One of the tallest animals that ever lived was a dinosaur called Brachiosaurus. It measured about 12 metres high and 25 metres long. It weighed more than 30 tonnes.

Brachiosaurus lived around 150 million years ago. Its great height allowed it to reach leaves on tall trees.

Brachiosaurus

A dinosaur called Sauroposeidon was probably even taller. So far scientists have only found a few of its neck bones, but they can work out from these how tall it is likely to have been.

Mosquitoes

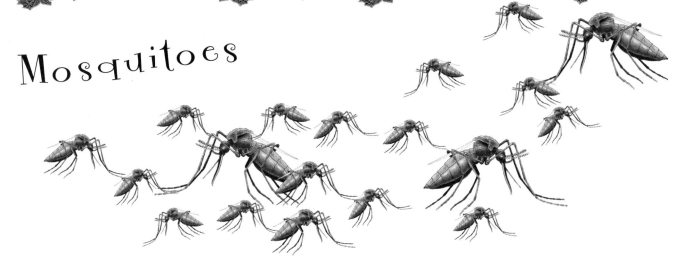

A mosquito has a needle-like mouth, called a **proboscis**, which it uses to pierce the skin and drink the blood of people or animals. Humans are easy to bite because we don't have thick fur or scales to protect us.

Cobra

How many people die of snakebites?

Several hundred people die from snakebites every year. In **tropical** countries, snakes often slither into people's homes. They will bite anyone who accidentally treads on them.

True or False?

The Brazilian wandering spider has the most deadly **venom** in the world.

Answers on page 31

What's the oldest living thing?

The bristlecone pine tree, found in the southern USA, may be the world's oldest living **organism**. Some bristlecone pines are almost 5,000 years old and still growing.

The trunk of a tree grows a new layer, or ring, every year of its life. Scientists can tell the age of a tree by counting the rings.

Usually, the animals and plants that live longest are the ones that grow most slowly.

Bristlecone pine tree

True or False?

The oldest sea creature is 300 years old.

Answers on page 31

What's the oldest land animal?

The longest-living land animals are the giant tortoises. They have been known to live for up to 200 years. A Galápagos tortoise named Harriet died in 2006 at the age of about 175.

Giant tortoises

The scientist Charles Darwin is said to have collected Harriet as a young tortoise in 1835.

What's the world's tallest tree?

The tallest tree is a coast redwood in California, which is 115.5 metres – that's around 65 times as tall as an adult human. Its exact location is kept secret to protect it from damage by tourists. In a forest, the tallest trees get most of the sunlight.

Coast redwood

Adult human

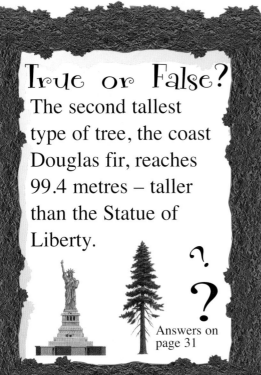

True or False?

The second tallest type of tree, the coast Douglas fir, reaches 99.4 metres – taller than the Statue of Liberty.

Answers on page 31

What's the biggest flower?

The Titan arum is a lily with the largest flower in the world. The flower can be 2.75 metres tall and 1.2 metres wide.

What's the smelliest plant?

The Titan arum also stinks like rotting flesh. The smell attracts flies. The flies then **pollinate** the flowers. The female flowers later become fruit. Birds eat the fruit and drop the seeds, and new plants grow.

Titan arum

What's the largest insect?

The largest beetle is the Hercules beetle, which can be 17 cm long. Male Hercules beetles have huge horns which they use to fight other males for a mate and for food. They live in hot, humid places, such as the rainforests of South and Central America.

What's the longest insect?

The longest insect ever measured was a giant stick insect. It was an amazing 55 cm long, including its outstretched legs. Many giant stick insects grow to over 30 cm long.

There are many different species of stick insect. They live in hot places such as the jungles of South-East Asia. Their stick-like shape gives them very good **camouflage**.

Stick insect hiding in leaves

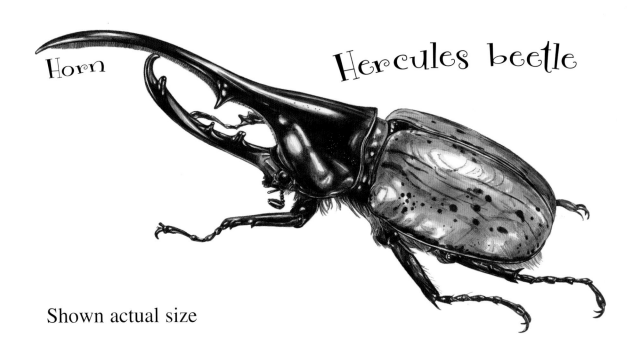

Horn

Hercules beetle

Shown actual size

What was the largest insect ever?

True or False?
The Goliath bird-eating spider from South America is the size of a dinner plate.

? ? ? ?

Answers on page 31

The largest insect that ever lived was a giant dragonfly called Meganeurid, which had a wingspan of 75 cm. It lived about 300 million years ago. These days insects cannot grow quite so big, because there is less oxygen in the air. Insects don't have lungs, so they can't get oxygen from the air as easily as other animals can.

What's the biggest bird?

The African ostrich is the world's tallest and heaviest bird, at 2.7 metres tall and 130 kg in weight. The giant moa of New Zealand and the elephant birds of Madagascar were much bigger, but these birds are now **extinct**.

Ostrich

Ostrich egg

Wandering albatross

What bird has the longest wingspan?

The wandering albatross, from the islands of the Antarctic ocean, has the largest wingspan – more than 3 metres from tip to tip. Albatrosses can glide great distances over the oceans without flapping their long, narrow wings. This helps them to save valuable energy.

Australian pelican

What bird has the longest bill?

The Australian pelican has the longest bill of any bird. The longest ever measured was 49 cm long. The bird grows up to 1.8 metres long, so the bill is almost a third of the bird's total length.

What's the most intelligent animal?

Of course, humans believe that they are the most intelligent species. The next most intelligent are the great apes – gorillas, orangutans, chimps and bonobos. But many animals are better at certain things than humans.

Squirrel

Pig

Ape

Dolphin

Squirrels sometimes trick other animals by pretending to hide food. Some dolphins have learned to use sponges to protect their noses from sharp corals. Some pigs are said to be good at video games!

Which animal has the largest brain?

Whales and elephants have bigger brains than ours. A human brain weighs about 1.5 kg, while that of an African elephant weighs about 7.5 kg. But if you compare the size of an animal's brain to the size of its body, then humans have the largest brains.

African elephant

Sperm whale

Human being

Humans are the only species capable of communicating by using spoken and written language – though some apes have been taught by humans to use simple sign language.

True or False?

Some birds use sticks to get at grubs hiding in branches. Answers on page 31

23

Who has the scariest teeth?

Sperm whales have long, narrow mouths filled with lots of pointed teeth for catching squid and fish. The sperm whale is one of the largest **carnivores** (meat-eaters) in the ocean, and its mouth is around 5 metres long. Its prey may include the giant squid, which can be over 12 metres long.

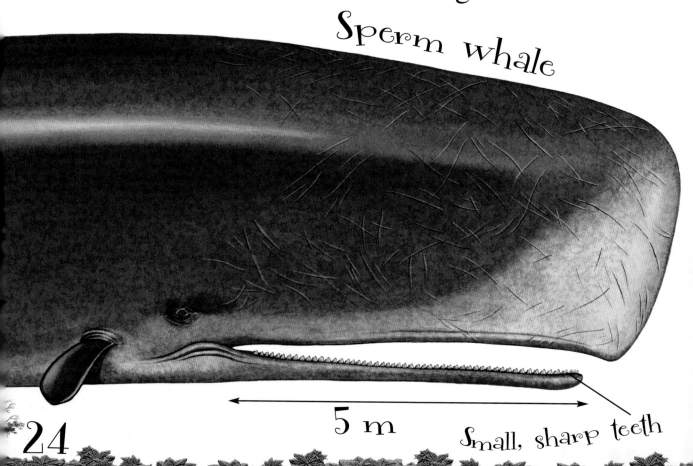

Sperm whale

5 m

Small, sharp teeth

True or False?

The giant squid has the largest eyes in the world. **?**

?

Answers on page 31

The hippopotamus has a huge mouth, complete with a set of very scary tusks. These tusks are actually long **canine teeth**. Male hippos have the longest tusks; they use them to fight other males. Although hippos are **herbivores** (plant-eaters), they are very aggressive and have been known to attack and kill people when they feel threatened.

Hippo

Tusks

What's the most endangered species?

Black rhino

The black rhinoceros is one of the world's most **endangered** species. It is hunted for its horns, which some people believe can be used to make medicine. Now there are only around 3,000 black rhinos left in the wild, and nearly all of these live in protected areas.

The giant panda is endangered because it can only live in a special habitat called bamboo forest. Because much of the bamboo forest has been destroyed, giant pandas now live only in a few mountain areas in China. Another problem is that pandas have very few cubs.

Giant panda

Tiger

Many species become extinct every year without many people noticing. These are often small animals or plants that are not so well known as bigger animals like tigers and pandas.

Tigers are endangered because people kill them or destroy parts of their habitat. Some tigers are hunted. Others are killed because they are dangerous to people and cattle. Many forests where tigers once lived have been cut down. There may now be more tigers in zoos and reserves than there are in the wild.

True or False?

The Scots pine is an endangered tree species. **? ?**

?

?

Answers on page 31

Who makes the longest land migration?

Migration means moving to a different place for part of the year. The longest migration on land is made by the caribou of North America. Each summer, thousands of caribou travel up to 5,000 km to the Arctic to look for food and to rear their young. In winter, they go back south.

Caribou

In Europe, caribou are called 'reindeer'

True or False?

The humpback whale travels 4,000 km in one trip.

Spur-winged goose

Every year, the spur-winged goose completes a gruelling migration from Europe and Asia to Africa and back again. The geese migrate when the weather turns cold and food becomes scarce.

Useful words

Camouflage Special markings, shapes or colouring on an animal that help it blend in with its surroundings.

Canine teeth The pointed teeth that are found one either side of the front teeth in humans and many other animals.

Carnivore An animal that eats mostly meat.

Endangered At risk of dying out.

Extinct No longer alive anywhere in the world.

Habitat The place where a particular type of plant or animal lives naturally.

Herbivore An animal that eats mostly plants.

Migration The movement of animals to a different part of the world for part of the year.

Organism A living thing.

Pollinate To help plants reproduce by carrying pollen from one plant to another.

Predator An animal that hunts and kills other animals for food.

Prey An animal killed and eaten by another animal.

Proboscis The needle-like mouth of a mosquito, used to puncture the skin of people and animals.

Rainforest A dense forest with high rainfall.

Species A group of living things that look alike, behave in the same way and produce young that do the same.

Tropical Having to do with the tropics – the hot, rainy area between the Tropic of Cancer and the Tropic of Capricorn.

Venom A poison produced by an animal.

Answers

Page 7   TRUE! Most types of bacteria are far too small to see with the naked eye. Thousands of them could fit on a pinhead.

Page 11   TRUE! Scientists think that the Seismosaurus reached 52 metres in length.

Page 13   TRUE! The bite of the Brazilian wandering spider causes swelling, fever and breathing problems. It can sometimes lead to death in people. The strong venom prevents the spider's prey from running away.

Page 15   FALSE! The oldest sea creature ever discovered was a clam over 400 years old.

Page 17   TRUE! The Statue of Liberty is only 93 metres tall. London's Big Ben is 96.3 metres.

Page 19   TRUE! The bird-eating spider is a kind of tarantula. It has a 30 cm leg span.

Page 23   TRUE! Galápagos finches prod with sticks to find grubs hiding in tree bark.

Page 25   TRUE! The giant squid's eyes can be up to 40 cm in diameter.

Page 27   FALSE! Scots pine is not endangered, but many other trees are. Big-leaf mahogany, for example, is cut down for its valuable timber and new trees are not always planted to replace the old ones.

Page 29   FALSE! The humpback migrates almost 5,000 km.

Giant tortoises

31

Index

(Illustrations are shown in **bold type**.)

Albatross

Giant stick insect